The Border Kingdom

The
Border
Kingdom

P O E M S

D. Nurkse

Alfred A. Knopf New York 2008

THIS IS A BORZOI BOOK
PUBLISHED BY ALFRED A. KNOPF

www.aaknopf.com

Knopf, Borzoi Books, and the colophon are registered trademarks of
Random House, Inc.

Library of Congress Cataloging-in-Publication Data
Nurkse, D., [date]
The border kingdom : poem / by D. Nurkse. — 1st ed.
    p.   cm.
"This is a Borzoi Book"—T.p. verso.
ISBN 978-0-307-26802-0
I. Title.
PS3564.U76B67 2008
811'.54—dc22   2008001884

Manufactured in the United States of America
First Edition

For Beth, with love

Limbo: the "second kingdom," adjoining paradise, from the Latin *limbus,* border

Contents

4 The Gods

I

The Age of
Great Crusades

. . . let us speak with the shadows . . .

Dante, *Purgatorio*

Jericho

Sometimes in a high window
a white curtain knotted against itself

gives a glimpse of the lovers
as they were before the war:

with great concentration and silence
they undo a mother-of-pearl snap

while a cat perched on the sill
looks down with burning eyes.

Albi

Because I could not admit
we know God through suffering
I was sealed up in the wall.
They left a gap in which my body
could curl like a fetus,
and a little sky, which they filled in
brick by brick, and perhaps
it troubled the masons
to be immuring a human being
because they whistled loudly,
a trowel shook, mortar spilt.
Yet it was a tight course.
I knew better than to press against it.
When the dark closed in
I lay listening to my pulse
louder, louder, and the distant voices
singing—I knew better
than to guess the words
or listen for my name.

Then I was the wall itself,
everything the voices long for
and cannot have—the self,
the stone inside the stone.

The Gate of Abraham

. . . [I] met an old woman with a bowl of flaming coals and a flask of water. She said that with the fire she intended to burn up paradise and destroy it, and with the water she would quench the fires of hell . . .

—Jean de Joinville, *Chronicle of the Crusades*

I

In the first weeks of the opening skirmish
King Louis was stranded in the sea-lanes at Damietta.
The sultan was garroted by his own guard.
Mercenaries melted away, nuncios
took to the high seas in a leaky skiff.
I was remanded to Acre with the clerics
to grow old among jugglers and goliards.
My life seemed huge, like a cloak too big,
after the narrow moment of killing.

At Michaelmas a knight with a suppurating wound
begged extreme unction and I confessed him.
I blessed him with two fingers, *ego te absolvo*.
His eyes rolled back, he coughed and stiffened,
but I could not remember a word of his sins.
My mind was humming with my own failure.

Perhaps I had escaped the bitterness of victory
for an intimate defeat, riddled with waiting.

In winter, the camp teemed with refugees,
spies, corrupted saints, rival chroniclers,
though nothing happened in Outremer
except doves volleying through dusty cedar
and a cricket temporizing inside a wall.

Evenings I longed for the lisp of Poitiers,
the sarcasm of the Angevin backcountry.
Wandering from barracks to barracks,
I met a toothless woman in the blue wimple
of Périgord, stumbling with a gourd and bowl.

I begged for a sip, and to warm my hands.
She agreed, but counted to herself,
staring at my Adam's apple. I dawdled
just for her company. She smelled of old age,
stale Burgundy, the thyme of my village.

She was in no mood for delay.
She pried my fingers from her hem,
picked up her burdens, and limped
toward the Gate of Abraham.

I warned her, that way is the desert.
Nothing there except stones and wind,
the mountains of the holy land like frayed silk.
Once you enter those names—Hebron, Moriah—
you will find only scripture, no hearth,
just darkness and the radiant sheen of ink.

She kept going. I watched until sundown,
when the glint of the coals began to waver.

From across the dry river the enemy prayer
rose, searing in its desire for God,
the counter-echoes, the renegade dogs,
at last the opposite stillness, deepening
as her steps receded.

Ben Adan

The American commanded me
in gestures, dig a hole.

He tossed me a shovel
but the blade had dulled
and the haft was splaying
so I had to rein in
that strange wild energy
as I opened the earth
to my shins, then my knees.

At thigh-depth I found
a layer of black loam
and a tiny blue snail
that seemed to give off light.

The agent called my name.
High above, he mimed
a man kneeling,
hands clasped in prayer.

He must have knelt himself
because I felt the muzzle pressed
against the shallow furrow
behind my left earlobe—
a part of my body
I never knew existed.
He pulled the trigger.

But I know
it is just a technique
to soften my resistance—

perhaps in a moment
he will lift me up
and hold me trembling,
more scared than I
and more relieved.

2

The Limbo of
the Fathers

In the Hold

After an unmeasured time as a stowaway
in the stifling void, listening to the waves,
the rats, the grains of wheat settling,
my father heard church bells
and knew he'd come to port.
When they rang past twelve
he was sure the war had broken out,
the world war that had been expected
all through childhood, for so long
tailors adjusted their chalk lines for it,
painters shaded it into the middle distance
like an unknown primary, preachers exhausted
the endings for their sermons;
now my father in the dark cubbyhole
that might be endless, or just a hair
larger than his ungrown body,
counts the coins in his sack,
the stitches in the gunny weave—
he takes his pulse, then having
no more real things, he counts
the members of his family, the chimneys
of his village, all the days
of his life in the old country.

Exile's Child

I asked my father
permission to kill a fly.
I came back and asked
—could I kill another?
He thought for a while
and said—No. Evening was taking
the sting off a family outing.
Along the beach, cousins
were charring meat. The waves
were turning an intense No-color.
I asked, was he in combat
in the old country? He said—No.
Then I was enraged at him,
feeling he was asleep, like the sand,
like the striped umbrella whose shadow
fell at right angles to night,
like my serious brother toting sums
in a leather-bound ledger. The flies alone
were awake, and their drone,
fainter than surf, was audible
only when I knelt and held my breath
stock-still by the banked coals.

The Cave Behind the Torrent

My father took me
to see the high waterfall
but I didn't want to go.
He thought I was afraid but in fact
I just didn't like waterfalls
or twilights or mist
or the approaching roar
or the long mossy path
suddenly intuiting a clearing—

I didn't like days
so when he cleared his throat
I said "put me down,"
when he stumbled
I said "carry me"—

he was defenseless
against my boredom
for I loved only him
and the smell of his skin
and his frayed plaid cuffs
with their shameless nacre buttons.

I loved his loneliness,
how thwarted his love of me
was, how I could channel it
and turn it off; the wall of water
glittering like stone
was just more prevarication.

The state had built a roped-in platform
from which to view dissolving rainbow wisps.
We stopped there. I cried.
He asked why. I cried louder,

and that was that twilight:
Why? *Wail.* Why? *Wail.*
Roar of current, little laminated captions
explaining the falls: gallons per second;
vertical drop; significant pioneers.

As my father read this information
I wriggled from his arms
and ran through the wall itself—
it was amazingly light

and there on the inside
I mimicked his voice
shouting my name.

When he fought his way
bitterly, warily, through the scrim,
I was just a ball of hate—

he was still living, I could not know
I was sick with happiness
and the gate had opened at one touch.

Driving to Canaan with My Father

Between Amado and Covered Wells
tiny frogs began looping
across the road and my father
slowed and started honking
furiously, adjusting the speed
of the wipers but the frogs
arrived thick and fast
from nowhere, perhaps
the dusty jack pine—

lucky it would soon be night
and we'd know them only
as a tremor in the high beams,
a series of faint blows: for now

we inched toward the peaks—
cruelly white, radiant with distance,
Mount Tabor, Mount Hebron, Cerro Dolor,
and beyond, the cloud fortresses:

who said we would live forever,
he and I, cautious, with the same face,
one lined, the other pudgy,
each swearing under his breath,
each flinching, each determined
to reach the border without speaking.

The Prize

When we came to the summit,
our father had one grape left.

We said, divide it.

But he refused.
He'd give it to the hungriest.

We fought then
on that narrow ledge,

the vineyards tilting
far below us—

who was most bereft,
loneliest, furthest from home.

As we rolled in each other's arms
we glimpsed a vacant sky,

the mountains of the border
that shine with their own light,

and the familiar dust
glittering with sweat.

The Anti-Death

In case we might lose Roger Rabbit
our mother bought three surrogates
and locked them in a drawer
high in the linen cabinet:

so when we left him
as if by accident
on a swing in the snowy park—

when the older children wrestled him
with shouts of joy from our embrace—

when we dropped him in the icy lake
and the rowboat would not turn back—

she produced him: here is your love
who was not vanquished but only sleeping
in paradise, in the white of the eye,
in the loneliness between words.

Sacrifice

How angry we were
at the stuffed bunny
for making us love it
night after night.

We ripped off an ear,
tore out the stuffing,
scattered it in handfuls,
prized out an eye
to roll in our palms.

The back, which we had never seen,
shone just as bright
as the staring pupil.

We licked our fingers
and teased the empty socket.

Night fell.
We listened for footsteps.

When they came
they were the same as ever,
just the blood beating in the mind,
but the silence was utterly new.

We entered it
as you might sneak through a door,
answered it, as if it were a voice—

yet it was just silence
and we could no longer change it
by laughter, tears,
or any silence of our own.

Practice

I owned a white Spaldeen
shaped exactly like a baseball
but entirely rubber,
fake seams and body
all of one piece,
and I hurled it
all morning at the fence post,
hoping to make the margin
I missed by narrower—
avid to conceive
an infinitely narrow space.

By noon I tried to imagine
the opposite; the post itself;
if I could re-create it
with absolute clarity
in my mind I might hit it.
But always at the point of release
when all my strength spilled
into that dark arc
I closed my eyes
against my will
and saw my father's face.

2

I hooked one finger
and let my wrist flutter
so all four seams
might meet the wind.
My sinker sailed sideways
into the blind spot.

I cradled rubber stitches
deep in my palm
but my curveball obeyed
an unknown will.

A snagged thumbnail
meant knuckleball,
drool made a spitball,
but each time the pitch
swerved from my intent
as if that variance
were my true skill.

3

At every hundredth miss
I took a step back—
from so vast a distance
failure was heroic.

4

Time, I thought,
I will use time
instead of the will.
Didn't I see that force
nowhere, and its consequence
in every blowing candy wrapper?

Wasn't I a stranger
at eight to *I* at seven?

Hadn't the round wailing sisters
changed to willowy shadows,
lost in the eye of the jump rope?

5

Dusk came and I was no closer,
but it was no longer *I* missing,
just the hour, the breeze, emptiness,
the peppery smell of the lindens,
a first tentative firefly
and its imperious pattern—

when the kitchen window lit
I felt relieved of a great burden
to see my father so clearly,
shivering, gray, stammering to himself,

mincing a clove of garlic
until it was fine and plural
as the gesture itself,

known frown and unknowable fear
no longer trapped inside my eyes.

The Adversary

Because I once committed
the sin without remission,
what I did to George Amapoulous
was not worth entering
in the book of judgment.

I put a pin
in his red and white football
and rather than popping
it slowly deflated
night after night,
growing a dent
like a template
for death's fist.

When he won at marbles
I whooped and cheered
until he looked ridiculous.

If he lost I cried
and showed a scar I had acquired
biting my thumb in the attic
in the obsessive slanted light
from three ventilation slats.

When he fell in love
I was ecstatic,
I could not sleep,

I trembled and fainted
until he doubted himself.

I threw his bicycle
in the Eunoe River,
praying it would float.

I wore his cap backwards.
I buttoned his shirt
with great suffering—

I had chosen him as my enemy
because he was small,
almost invisible in the tall grass
that summer my father died.

2

My crime was to stab a shadow
in a dream, with a penknife
with five tools: nail file,
can opener, tweezer, corkscrew,
father-killer.

I allied with alien powers—
Plutonians, disguised as white ants,
racing in tight circles
according to a pact
the mind makes with broken things,

Uranians, who assume the form
of flies and walk upside down

on the roofs of coffins
and enter the eye itself,

Saturnian caterpillars
who weave a delicate thread,
unimaginably strong,
out of spilt blood.

3

My father whom I loved
lay in a hinged box
under a white blanket
that rose and fell
in the breeze from the fan

and George Amapoulous
came ambling home from softball
with his bat over his shoulder
and his glove perched on it,
humming to himself
a song that would end
in mid-breath.

August Snow

My father wanted to climb Mount Moriah
and we refused to go
unless it was understood
we were going against our will—
unless we could climb by suffering,
dragging ourselves step by step
through the boxwood glade,
withheld birch, glinting ash, oak bent
to the will of the south wind—

that was our secret,
denial, denial, we were children,
above all we wanted to be with him
above the tree line where the lakes
are dark as the pupil of the eye
and hold massive unmoving clouds
and the mouths of silvery wary carp.
We wanted to descend to the valley
at dusk, and shit and wipe ourselves
on the fat rhododendron leaves—

but he would not let us go
unless it was in delight
so we watched him
trudge off in the dawn wind,

all day we stared
at that faint snow-dusted peak

sometimes hidden by clouds,
sometimes a cloud itself,

and when night fell
it was just darkness
and no longer contained him.

3

The Limbo of
the Children

Nights in a Border Town

You asked why I was shaking.
I explained, it was the train
to Martirios, that left
a gold thread across the ceiling.

A cock crowed in Windfall
but our room was still dark.

I think there was no barrier
between us then: no world,
no other world, just nakedness

and the pupil of the eye
slowly becoming visible.

Hitching to Mount Hebron

I

We waited under the black oak
and after five minutes
or an hour, we were too just-married
to tell time, a blue-gray DeSoto
with its lights still on
slowed, we gasped
and grabbed our possessions—
knapsack, water bottle,
two A & P bags—but the driver
mirror-glanced, sped up,

2

and we ran a few feet,
kicked a pebble back in place,
resumed watching the heat sheen
waver on that camber
between pine and ash
where the road was;
once, you reached over
to pick a polka dot beetle
from my neck—brilliant blue,
with red eyes—I had never seen one

3

except in dreams, and felt nothing:
the sun was rising, the leaves
changed from being leathery shields
to almost transparent, we sensed
the first claims of the great heat

4

and we unfolded our map
of Cerro Dolor, the mountains
indicated by a funnel of convex lines,
the granitic passes by)(,
the boreal forest a green cross-hatching;
we wondered, were we in such a zone,
and tried consciously to feel lost
among those squiggle-roads
marked - - - - for impassable in winter

5

as we are lost now in days,
and in succession a white Impala
with tinted windows, a Willys,
a high-finned Edsel, a red Pierce-Arrow
roared past: we tried to fold the map
and stick out our thumbs with composure
but the berm shimmered with settling dust

6

so we forgave each other
and made a little sign
BORDER RANGE from waxy sandwich paper
glued with plum juice
onto the back of our notebook,
propped it carefully
with a forked stick, and made love

7

right behind the tall grasses
next to the slim black stream,
very cautiously and politely,
listening for brakes, removing
only pants and hats, then we lay

8

watching the high anvil clouds
drifting from Peru toward Lapland
while a small fat hummingbird
with a heartless bright eye
circled us, zipping in spurts,

9

and if we could borrow
that backwards flight
we would still be in the foothills
where the snowcaps are too close
to be visible, still waiting,
sharing the last dab of peanut butter
and the last sip of thermos instant
before we drink from the spring itself.

Canaan

How the mind wound up the doves
and sent them volleying
over the shepherds' low fences.

When the tap leaked
the mind said *drip,*
if a dog barked
the mind murmured *echo,*
and when the lovers moaned
the mind gasped a name.

Mount Moriah hovered
like a cloud in the north.
The river glinted like a hinge
long before daybreak.

Abraham had lent us that stone house
with warped blue shutters.

In his dusty pear orchard
ladders were nailed to every tree.

We were voices then—now
we are signs on the blank page.

At High Falls

1

We married by the falls, fell asleep,
and the child was born. Joy, exhaustion.

We taught her names for the river:
endless, merciless, oxbow,
alluvial, thwarted by cobalt,
covered with a fine dust of dead bees
moving as if by command south.
She made those sounds her way,
all verbs and vowels. We coaxed her
to walk along the banks, and pointed out
rills, riprap, a net of ripples
from a snagged pine, splash of a bass
against the current, the current itself
like a sheen or the white of the eye.
She dawdled, repeating those words
—*Anduren, Itaglio*—in a language
she invented, with our accent,
but without the intimate failure.

2

Each of us would see the world only once
in a finite sequence, each of us
knew a few stars—Aldebaran, Arcturus—
and assumed there were names
for the others, and no names

for the reflections that glittered
brighter each summer,
so we held hands bitterly,
certain that time was against us,
and the mind, and the veering wind.

3

In a dream you showed me
a moth walking on the surface,
almost indignantly—one stippled wing
was soaked, and would drag it
south, yet it kept marching
against the current. We were sure
we would not wake.

4

The cat studied us from every corner
of that shuttered house, inventing thresholds
even in a heap of pillows.

A migrating hawk memorized us,
wheeling, and left its faint cry
in the ribs of the brass bed.

5

Dead catfish appeared, belly-up,
trailing snarled whiskers,
and the child was wary,
old enough to name us: *mask, dart.*

Summer was invincible.
We looked over our shoulders
for a flashlight on the opposite shore.

Our last hope was a grievance
so we might remain, a broken promise,
a smooth glistening oyster shell
we refused each other, though the full moon
was contained there, and the extinct stars
that burn inside the mind.

Mount Tabor

We passed a willow forest
whose springy moss floor
was too green to step on,
elusive scrim of birch,
lichen-scarred oak roots
with a high breathing canopy,
then moraine, bare screes;
there wind had mined the granite
that crumbled under our boots.

We were carrying the child
so she might see the summit,
passing her between us
because sleep made her heavy.

The breeze turned blunt
and sidereal. We stopped
at a kettle lake and washed.
That water was so cold
it seared us. We told each other,
one more hour, but the pass
hung suspended, crazy high.

We promised not to raise our eyes again,
confined to each other's tracks.
By noon we had trudged
beyond the echo of our footsteps
into deep sky; ridge, clouds,
laboring hawk wing; suddenly
the air was below us.

We pointed and told the child
Mount Hebron, Mount Moriah

as if there were a correspondence
between the story we had been telling her
as we climbed—*sacrifice, freedom*—
and those ferrous shoulders
glinting with black snow:
ravens drifted like cinders:

a plaque, a circle of stones, a cairn:
we placed one more pebble on it—
we had to hunt for one small enough—
we offered the child that honor
but she was bored and mouthed *no.*

We plunged toward Lorimer
and the valley opened beneath us,
roads like threads in a reversed coat,
slim waterfall, manicured vineyard,
fire ponds like nailheads.

Always we glanced back at our climb,
victory raised like a barrier,
cloud-wrapped, as if the child
were still poised at that height

though she slept in our arms
and the one who did not carry her
felt the weight of the mountain.

The Border Range

We came down from the little mountains
once every few weeks
for a sack of rice, or lard, or candles,
or just to talk for a moment
with the old man in the paper-bag hat
who lounged at the door with a fly whisk.

We would complain about each other:
he's bitter, he wants so much;
what she has she doesn't want;
and we'd brag of the harshness
of that plateau, the splendor
of Andromeda, the absolute silence.

Sometimes we boasted
of the waterfall, the whirlwinds,
the downy soft-pinioned owl
drifting in daylight
with a hole in his voice,
the immense cliffs—

and that is all anyone knows
of those years of marriage,
labor, voluntary poverty:
those mountains were perfectly flat
and exist only as a little rip
where the map was folded once too often.

Return to Underhill Road

Strangers live in huge cities,
they get married, they love each other,
it scares them how they love each other,
it happens in words, in signs,
and also somewhere else,
a place they can't reach—

so we drive home from the airport
in the great heat and the domino players
hunch over their card tables
at the corner of Euclid and Gates.

A woman wrings a shirt from a high window.
Two children are locked in a game:
one teeters in a thrower's stance,
one stares at a cloud, openmouthed:

everything wants to wake up,
water gushes from hydrants,
the frisbees would love to glide
straight out of the frisbee dream
as out of a frame in the comics—

so we negotiate the rusty locks,
undress each other, lie naked,
our bodies are the great roads,
but it happens somewhere else—
in the dead rainbows of spilt oil,
the hauteur of twilight clouds,

the desire of passing cars
to reach their unknown destination,

while the child in the next room
swathed in her crib
makes every sign in every alphabet
and sings every sound in every language
until it will become a story—

two rooms, one marriage,
this trance, happiness.

The Child

I lie swaddled,
trapped in this wail,
and she brings me
sponge, spoon, plastic key.
So she assuages me.
She lends intent to the cry,
my intent. She creates
a cause, desire.

Once she has power to soothe,
I have power to relent.

◆

With my thumb
I make the sign
for sunlight on a wall
in late summer in a vast city.
I am naked, small as a shoe.

◆

I practice Kikuyu click language
and the Japanese *p*
blown across the lips.

◆

I imitate her face.
It is a great labor
to follow all its moods.
They are my suffering,
my delight, my abandonment.

◆

No one calls me *you*.
I am addressed in the third person
as if I were sideways to the world.

◆

I am singing, but gradually
I can isolate a cadence,
how the voice rises half a tone
just before the pause.

Still there is no gap
between words and days.

Always the cat
lands on the sill,
brindle tail like a flag.

I cannot find the frame,
the way to separate myself,
silence, since it is gone
as soon as I summon it.

◆

I make the sign
for the cat's disappearance
into its own rapt eyes,
for the cloud in the mirror,
the ability of the body
to be contained
in the crook of an elbow,
the vinegary smell of the armpit.

There is something small
that arrests me in a word,
a seed of breath.
I spit it out again and again
until it becomes my father.

❖

Is this language as impenetrable
as the old roar of blood
and close thudding heart?

❖

At night she cinches the curtain
and I make the room dark
with the pupil of my eye.

Lament for the Makers of Brooklyn

Where is Policastro the locksmith now?
Half-blind, he wore two pairs of glasses
held together with duct tape,
and arranged hasp, tongue, eye screw
on a deal table—everything ordered
by resistance, scrim of rust,
flange, interlocking wheel,
name, distance from the body;
afterward the key turned
for you but not for me.
He charged us $11.39.
We tipped and he smiled bitterly.
Perhaps he would have smiled the same
if we'd paid the flat amount—
perhaps he had a bitter smile—

Simon his cousin fixed the windows,
assembling mossy torpedo-shaped weights
and flat-linked chain spliced to steel cord,
beveled panels of the embrasure
that fitted into themselves
to make a plane, a sheen
over invisible labor—later
the window lodged at a cant
for you, and for me slid open
onto a street of moving vans.

Mr. Fuchs with his green wrench
consulted a brass thermometer
and opened the hydrants in the great heat.
He stood behind the plume of spray
as with a young bride in a lace veil—
where are the children who ran after Spaldeens
and found them floating toward Africa in the gutter,
glinting with gasoline rainbows?

Where is Vera B. Wick
who raised Clarence and Latisha
in a room no bigger than a white glove,
and never looked up from Revelation
during the war against fear?

What became of Clarissa Green
who organized Blue Forge,
preaching to Croatians
from a dictionary in her lunch box,
bargaining with Yemenites
via a Berlitz phrase book wrapped in foil:
shouldn't this life be easier?

Diagnosed with MS, she took on Bridal Shower
where no union had ever been allowed,
where the carders drool from mercury—
she marched straight up to the guardhouse
and announced *I have an appointment.*

What happened to Sister Violet
who drew pyramids on the chalkboard,

her hands shaking with desire
for a lover dead at Khe Sanh?

Who remembers South Wind the numbers runner
who nudged me in the men's room
of the He's Not Here Cafe
and told me, zipping and buttoning,
I'm going to meet the sweet one?
That winter he was found
in the trunk of a green Impala
on an access road in the marshes.

Where is Thelma, who owned the pigeons
that made enormous whirling obelisks
and spires, only to disappear
with a single will toward Bayonne?

2

Once I met a crossing guard from the old neighborhood
at a side table in Starbucks.
She blew on her steamed milk
and tapped her fingers to 'N Sync.

Once I met a pipe fitter
who had invested in Power Disk
and made a fortune, and lost it:
so deep in debt he still walked
with the wary nonchalance
of a poor man become the center of the world—

he wore a belt with a mother-of-pearl buckle
and his initials wrought as twisting snakes:
he confided to me, perhaps this was the afterlife,
surely he died from a stray bullet
in that year when the children
began crying for bottled French water.

3

Remember how we lay in the great heat
in our walk-up on Seeley Street
between the immense park and the huger cemetery?
The neighbor's radio played *Fearless Heart*
but whenever we tried to listen to our own music
a plane passed, circling La Guardia—

how desperate we were to sense a shift in power
in the mourning dove's quavering voice,
a new age in the humming clock—
Kennedy, Johnson, Ford, Carter,
Reagan, Bush, Clinton, Bush,
constant whoosh of traffic
passing to the Island;

as if even our bodies, naked, linked
by a stray arm, were time,
and the candor of our love
confined us in childhood.

4

Last night I met the knife grinder
whose cart with its infuriating bell
jolted among the elms
riddled with lovers' names
in the dead of summer,
so that wives left their dark houses
and came to him and offered
the carving knives from their trousseaux—

and he described to me, with a flicker
of his tiny nicotine-stained hands,
how he cut the little holes in the straw hat
so his horse's ears would be comfortable,
and how he honed the blade
so keen you could not feel it cut.

The Deferment

1

To avoid that draft
I studied books on headaches.
I stayed up nine nights.
I found a headache so perfect
it did not need a body.

2

I sliced a tiny sliver
off my trigger finger.

I prepared a razor,
basin, and napkin.
I closed my eyes.

The cut part vanished
as when you slap a fly
and search your palms
for a trace of wing.

3

To forget that carnage
I married, grew old,
raised children, was loved

and long before dawn
lie listening to the rain
and the stillness between drops.

Rosal

I / THE VISIT

Many identical metal detectors
and the guards in strange moods.
One cups a hand for your change,
lets it spill, and fingers his gun
while you bend to scoop up pennies.
Another is reading Revelation
and waves you on without a pass.

Is it your shoe that triggered the beep?
You will pad in socks, a yellow nail
poking from the seam.

Nine gates where clerks ask
how did you get to this point?
as if there had been choices.

As at the entrance to a concert,
a boy in shades stamps your wrist—
here the ink is invisible.

You will walk these dim corridors
while a megaphone calls your name
gently, then in anger, then panic.

Still a trustee will usher you
through ribbon wire and sensors.

And there in a floodlit cell
Rosal is drawing keys
on a scrap of paper—

ancient keys, to enormous locks,
though here the doors are opened
only by a beam of light:

so little margin, soon
he will draw on his own hand,
his wrist, his belly,

then the music will blast,
all bass and reverb,
and no one left to dance.

2 / THE RECORD

We made a chapbook
and called it <u>My Life</u>
(underlined twice)
(nothing happens after prison)
but the staples were confiscated
    —weapon, weapon—
and held in a safe at Command:
there the brass-bound book
lies open to a marked page.

3 / PAROLE

Three months I practiced
my reunion with Marla
in the kitchen in Rego Park:
it happened exactly as in dreams:

a kiss, the promise,
the red-check tablecloth,
the cat watching indignantly,
a candle, the deep kiss,

except we had a few sips of Hennessy
and her brother came by
and commented on punks from prison.
The cat slithered under the credenza.

Then that three-month dream
fueled a drink, another drink,
a hard laugh, a soft laugh,
a shove, and I was back
at Command, nine-to-fifteen,

staring at the whitewashed wall,
hearing myself talk
loud, louder, softly,
then never again.

4 / INCIDENT AT IRA CROSS

It hurts to see it
even with the white of the eye—

everything has a beginning and end
except the beating—

but a roll of toilet paper
sails blazing over the grillwork,
splaying in midair:

even in Section Eight, Isolation,
someone unknowable owned a match.

5 / LOCKDOWN

A glove searches the anal cavity.
Is there really a drug
this bloody, or a weapon
so infinitesimally small?

6 / MALE MINOR DETAINEE

Rosal hung himself
on Rikers Island
with a nylon sock—

how could it hold him
so securely in death
when the whole block shook
with the roar of jets
circling La Guardia?—

to be free and walk
without meeting men's eyes
across the bridge to the city.

Two Small Empires

In those snowy streets—
little caffè macchiato bistros
with gold lettering and cloudy windows,
car services, storefront churches,
a failed Goodyear warehouse—
the Bloods and Crips were fighting,

making their presence known
by subtle distinctions:
backwards Yankees cap,
Mets cap sideways,
Calvin Klein jeans.

Almost no onlookers were hurt
though the killers were children
and sometimes fired at random,
pulled in tight circles
by the weight of their silenced Glocks.

It was the third year of our marriage.
Eight months pregnant, you stumbled
from Charybdis to Cairo Palace,
hunting for cloves, anchovies, endives.

You had to gain weight.
I cooked vats of soup:
crème de sour cream,
bouillon with silver dollars of fat.

We took care never to mention
how happy we were
in those long evenings—
rented bed set, Levolor blinds,
blue sleet in a gated window.

At dawn another siren,
a woman rending her black veil,
struggling to find a seam
as the flashing lights faded.

The Shelter

You breathed in my ear
and we began waiting,
invincible in our armor
of light sweat.

There in the subbasement
we kept a water bed,
a radio, nineteen dented cans
of Del Monte wax beans,
the coil to a flashlight,
an atlas, and a diary.

We missed each other
most when we came—
then we rolled apart
fingertips touching,
and practiced being victims
of a war in the mind.

How we loved that world,
its smell of must,
its darkness, its single light.

4

The Gods

Giants Versus Angels

Willie Mays slipped out of the shadows,
the arc of the fly hewing
to the contour of his gesture.
That effortless catch zipped chaos
and I made it again in my mind.
I borrowed his shy grace.

I was Bob Gibson shaking off a sign,
Koufax painting the inside corner,
Maris reading a rotating seam,
and I introduced subtle variations—
Mantle's grand slam inched foul
for I was misfortune and the breeze.

I was Jimmy Cannon pounding
on a lyre-shaped Smith-Corona
behind a wall of blinding cameras.
When the bleachers erupted
I was that roar—*fury of the dead:*
in the first inning of childhood
I peeked in my father's bedroom
and the blue screen captured me.

❖

I could never leave that game
except once, when I was DiFusco,
paunchy mid-reliever bound for the minors,
hurling lame heat in a remote bull pen.

Then I caught the eye of an arthritic pigeon
scrounging in the dust, felt a twinge
in my ankle, and froze in mid-delivery
while the bird stared, shrugged, and took wing.

How longingly I watched it recede
past concession stands, a maze of gates,
the broad avenue strewn with entry stubs,
toward freedom and the streets of home.

Autopoiesis

A little evening crept
into the poet's Bausch & Lombs;
he polished them
with a chamois scrap
until they were invisible.

He took a sip of Perrier,
admiring his breath
in the vinyl cup.

This next fragment, he said,
is longer than life itself,
but it is the shortest lyric
I ever conceived.

So the voice engulfed us,
whirling us to the past;
when silence claimed us

we waited in that endless line
to grace our crisp new books
with the fissure of his name.

As we inched forward
we touched each other
on the thigh, the cheek,
almost by accident,

as if to remind ourselves
how it had been to be alive—
pure fire.

We admired the halo of down
around that august backlit ear,
the fury of the blue-veined hand
scribbling *self self self,*

and we whispered *love your work*
to the rain in the empty street.

A Marriage in Belmont

Sometimes we would walk
into the cobalt-blue TV,
take off our clothes,
and hang upside down like bats.

Then we would watch
from the spindled elm leaves
where names are sealed
with sap and nail polish.

Fascinated we would watch.

The Airedale slipped
his long leash of *dog*
and the cat curled into herself
like night in a dream

but what are those cries?

—Darling, they are the children
riding their wide-tired bicycles

with great care through the geraniums
we suffered so to plant.

—Darling, they are you and I
making love in a glass box
lest we find ourselves
alone and voiceless in the fire.

Late Summer

When the rain woke me
I no longer knew
and had to remind myself:
this is darkness,
that is the wineglass,
this is the blowing curtain,
that's the immense city,
it's late in my life
but early in August,
this is my wife
naked in my arms.

Picnic by the Inland Sea

We understood we were hurtling into space
at eighteen miles per second, clouds of atoms
charged and polarized, each alone
in the abyss, and you wore your summer dress.
The light under the poplar was mottled
but the shade of the pines was feathered.
We were bundles of self-canceling voices—
flight and response, punishment and reward,
hostile adoration, panic and certainty—
from long before the Bronze Age,
yet we made our own promises
by suppressed coughs or sneezes
and sat a little apart
but sometimes our eyes brushed.
We sipped Montepulciano from a paper cup
until the bottom darkened
but still it was not evening,
still the world was ending,
always we resented the breeze
for choosing and marking us,
still a song too short to sing
moved two famished sparrows
like pawns from branch to branch.

Three Naps at Walker Point

I slept, when I woke
I had built this cabin
with its shade garden,
flagstones, and screened porch
overlooking Burnt Coat Harbor.

I dozed, when I came to myself
we were middle-aged, our children
called from an inner room—
you stirred and tiptoed out,
agile as the breeze.

I drowsed and at twilight
I remained in the dream,
in the cursive slope of the letters
that would contain it, caught
in the maze of reflected masts,

so I bit back panic and listened
for the bell from the ocean.

The Missing

We filled the streets,
squinting upward, shading our eyes,
searching for the towers,
or more planes, or rescue choppers,
and a great silence built

until a girl whispered, *blood*.
She asked her lover to stand still,
used his back for a drawing board
and wrote on a paper bag
Give Blood—instantly

a line formed, then many lines,
twelve blocks east to Bellevue,
eighteen north to Saint Vincent.
We chose one and waited,
gossiping with our neighbors.

We had a place, a function,
something invisible inside us
was needed desperately; we watched
with envy and deep longing

as the rare blood types
strode toward the head of the line
calmly, swinging their arms,
commandos to the rescue.
Then the word came back,
              no wounded.

After a Bombing

1

Lovers who had separated
asked *are you okay?*
and reconciled.

Fathers who had abandoned
their children whispered
Thank God you were in Queens.

The man who was late
because of a lost key
felt good fortune on his shoulders,
a tower he'd have to carry,

the woman who called in sick
wandered deeper into fever,
looking for suffering,
for a spring to drink from,

and the children drew the plane,
sticking out their tongues, pressing
hard with crayons, never looking up,
as if they'd seen it all their lives:

the tower—a huge box:
the fire—an orange flower:

God—a face with round eyes
watching from the margin:
the sun with nine spokes:

the fireman in his smudged hat
running with outstretched arms
up a flight of endless steps
that veered suddenly off the page.

Survivors

The one we loved
lay trapped under the rubble
and we heard tapping,
first late at night,
then in the silence
between sirens, then always
in that city half-deserted
at the onset of winter.

In the factory whose windows
blazed with evening—
in the immense theater
before the curtain rose—

in the unmade bed
we kept returning to
because loneliness
shook us like leaves.

It is the pulse, love, you said,
that maddening relentless code.

In the Year of Circular Marches

A young girl on the train
was handing out leaflets,
shaking a drunk awake,
reading the text to a panhandler,
making him repeat it,
confronting a nun, a security guard.

Two lovers were clasped
and she stood over them
rocking with their motion,
until they separated
and rubbed their eyes.

Good luck, I said,
I expected her to grin back,
but she was tired,
I was one less obstacle
and she moved on
staggering a little, a vein
bulging in her calf.

I could read her lips
since I knew what she was saying:
the next four days are crucial:
then the train went aboveground,

a brickworks, whirling snow,
she was gone and the beggar
cleared his throat and announced
my house in Kew Gardens burned

and the riders had changed:
off-duty soldiers, National Guard
stamping slush from their boots—

the pattern of the treads
was intricate and dazzling
at the point of melting—

and we could almost see our faces
wavering, picking up speed.

Liberation in Winter

We speak of the bombing
but it may never happen.
We imagine the two planes,
spotter and payload,

glinting north of Alpha Centauri.
We watch the rain of warheads
spiraling in moonlight
but they may never land.

This crusade, this carnage,
this rule of strange weapons—
the flinch, the sigh, the glance away—
may be just a faux pas between lovers

who lie naked, an inch apart,
in the stepwise shadow of the blinds.

Letter from Solange

1

She writes: we have been invaded by images.
We don't know where they come from.
We suspect there is no artist.
They have found a way to replicate themselves.
Usually it is the body of love.
An enigmatically smiling lower lip.
A closed eye, delicately veined.
A long sinuous eyelash.
A male sex, wrinkled and solemn, surprisingly small.
The vagina, and a freckle.
A nipple. The curve of the inner thigh.
The hollow just above the hips,
backlit with a sheen of sweat.
Sometimes a landscape.
A street in autumn, yellow maple leaves
whirling in midair, in the middle distance.
The house with dark windows. Or just its gates.

2

She continues: stories have come between us
like wisps of smoke.
He was born in Basel in 1956.
She found another lover.
Davison waited in dark glasses outside the stadium.
He brought her a jar of pansies, blue almost black.
The planes passed toward China, leaving faint contrails.

They are fragments that suppose a whole.
They have strange confidence in their resolution,
in that throat-clearing word "arc."
They console us, though they are a labyrinth,
a stinging fatigue, a lifelong burden.
But there is no author.
In the hush of early afternoon
before the street fills with children,
when the sun curls like a starfish
on the scalloped wallpaper,
you might glimpse one making itself up.

3

The weapons destroyed each other.
The election voted against itself.

When I wrote "the middle distance"
I meant: we gave up that refuge.
We abdicated voluntarily.
We lured our enemy into our house.

4

All summer we lay in the narrow bed,
she writes, the light passed over us
in great rafts, in silent chords,
and nakedness stunned us.

Today I felt a hollow beside me
shaped like the body, and smoothed it flat.

I scribbled this letter and sealed it.
Though the streets were still empty,
a little fog at the corners,
a few sleepless soldiers pitching dice,
I mailed it, she writes,
yet the story will not stop telling itself.

5

The latest updates insinuate
you have given yourself
to suffering, a story
in which there is no one
except God and no end but paradise—

they say the war will never end now,
there is no one left to surrender,
the enemy is just a swirl of pollen.

6

I walk home against the flood of children
who lope silently, doggedly, frenziedly, absurdly late.
Their satchels bang against their thighs
and the long trail of maps, notes, tests,
drawings of rainbows, reports on the Peloponnesian War,
flutters in the middle distance
where you and I grew old.

Parousia

When we were in the same room as the gods
there was little to say.
Do you like twilight? Do you need the touch
of the other's body—the absolute other?
Mostly we stared at their wingtips
which were burnished
and stamped with strange almost-holes.
How could they stand the suffering
of the fly trying to walk
across the sheen and camber
of a brimming Campari glass?
It would happen to us,
but it was they who had to watch
and watching is hardest.
Only a breath away,
they showed no desire to vanish
though the silences that opened
were volatile as the shadows
of the last exhausted dancers.
Which do you prefer—time or lightning?
We could hear the clink
of the chandelier trying to work its way
loose from the vaulted ceiling,
a cello tuning sharp in an inner room,
and curried almonds being gobbled—

that was us, our voracity,
but the gods said nothing:
their politeness is like their love:
glass wall between us and midnight.
We pitied them. It is not safe
on that side of eternity.
Worse than watching is waiting
while the waiters sweep up the party hats
and dark lights of snow
tumble in the immense gilt-framed mirror.

The Gods

Remember the old Commodore Theatre
in North Brooklyn on the border
of Williamsburg and Greenpoint?

A famished calico cat
wailed in the love scenes,
swishing against our shins,
marking us obsessively.

Remember the ABC Hotel
hidden over a storefront chapel
on a street of Jiffy Lubes?

One night we undressed each other,
slipped under boiled sheets,
and found a used rubber.

How would we ever sleep
with the heat pipes clanging?

Remember those passions
we wore like T-shirts:
GRIEF RESENTMENT GUILT DELIGHT?

◆

There in the past
we walk the icy streets
of the Projects alone,
accusing each other—

aren't we complicit
with the bland pounding music,
don't we want absolute power
if only over each other?

◆

And we stare at the lit windows
in which the gods are changing diapers,
dusting, scouring, or just dozing,
lost in their endless books—

as if we might still see
our future there, in that room
carved from pure light

where a sleepless child
searches for a city
hidden by a cloud of breath.

A Child in Brooklyn

She stood on the dictionary
to reach the mirror
and whispered to that white cloud
look: I'm me.

In another room
her father licked his finger
to leaf through a divorce decree
with nineteen codicils:

as you were before:
independent lives:
child remains happy:
time is divided in two
but child stays in one body:

independent lives, happiness:
why didn't we think of that
before it became law?

In another room
her mother in a large white hat
was packing a valise,
thumbing through postcards,
throwing out an ocean liner,
keeping a waterfall
with an arrow and the words
wish you were still here.

The huge books had been sorted.
The ones with sad endings would be kept
because the settings were so beautiful:
Ischia, Bari, the vineyards of Zion.

Never before had the city been so vast
or the war so remote
or the bombing so precise.

It seemed it had already happened
and been encoded into computers
but no, it was just human life,

if you thought *up* you rose
on tiptoe and *down* you huddled
on the buckling lino.

If you thought *sparrow*
a small shadow darted by
self-important behind the frosted glass
but if you thought
here I start it was over.

So the child drew the letter *I*
in the heart of the cloud
and there she saw a fiery counselor

who shines now she and we are gone.

Leaving Hawk Mountain

I longed to teach the child
the pinheaded oscillating glide
of the turkey buzzard,
nimble serene accipiter,
chunky-tailed spiraling buteo
and scissoring merlin,
osprey lofted like a spark,
bold V of a harrier
locking the dusk

and I wanted her to mimic them
with key mistakes, running in circles
until she tripped and lay looking up
at the first faint stars
and I could comfort her.

But that was long ago.

Square stems of wild mint
rattled in the breeze
from the river of stones.

The hummingbird had built a nest
of thimbleweed and down
and let it fill with pollen.

A last busload of families
surged past me, Kodaks poised,
children balking and preening,
eyes bright and oblique,
solemn rapt father
explaining the night sky.

Lorimer

I traveled all night
in these dark foothills—
once or twice a porch lamp,
a ticking screen, a dog
wailing dutifully—

but I never came to Windfall
or saw my father's face.
Loneliness of white lines.
Can just a padlock close the mines?

Now it's morning
and the little churches gleam
like dice across the valley.
I'm so tired of gauge and wheel

and the way the Esso signs
light from within
with a hostile radiance
that fades when I arrive

in Lorimer, just north of Canaan:
sheen of winter wheat
crouched as if to spring,
slim high waterfall

and a tethered jug,
cross scratched on a stone,
hush of the white farm

with its yard full of hinges—
crooked fence, leaky pump,
guard dog jerked back
by a voice or a chain.

My father is lonely,
buried at La Cruz,
and still the bees
zoom around the staved-in hive.

Grafton

Hardly had I died
when I found myself driving
on a dirt road north of Canaan.

It was almost night or morning
but you could sense the fog
climbing through orchards
up the flanks of a mountain.

A system of fences receded—
perhaps a riding school—
and lush fields fell back
where the corn stood tense
and absent, like soldiers.

The forest asserted itself.
Beech and ash, then pine.
White moths shot by like sparks.

If this is limbo, I asked
(your presence was beside me),
why are there so many signs—
Lorimer Six Miles; Farm Machinery?

As always, you answered with silence,
but you touched my cheek
so gently I could feel
the whorl of your fingerprint.

A plywood Holstein cutout
swayed on a rusty chain.
The branches lifted.

As always, I could not desist
and pestered you under my breath:

Why do the porch lights
guard these small towns
so jealously?

Why do the lupines
nestled on the cropped berms
give off such darkness?

Why do the round pools,
hoses dangling at the rims,
tremble as if a child swam there?

Acknowledgments

Thanks to the editors of the following magazines, in which poems in this book first appeared (place names are changed in some titles):

The American Poetry Review: "Rosal"

Barrow Street: "The Gate of Abraham," "The Deferment"

The Cortland Review: "Return to Underhill Road," "In the Year of Circular Marches"

Epiphany: "Sacrifice"

Field: "Ben Adan," "Two Small Empires"

Hanging Loose: "Driving to Canaan with My Father," "The Adversary," "Nights in a Border Town"

Hunger Mountain: "The Gods"

The Jewish Daily Forward (newspaper): "After a Bombing"

The Kenyon Review: "Hitching to Mount Hebron," "Survivors," "Letter from Solange"

The Literary Review: "Jericho," "Canaan," "The Border Range," "Lament for the Makers of Brooklyn," "Grafton"

Lumina: "A Child in Brooklyn"

The Manhattan Review: "The Prize," "The Anti-Death," "Practice," "Mount Tabor," "The Child," "Giants Versus Angels," "Lorimer"

Nerve (Internet magazine): "The Shelter"

The New Yorker: "Picnic by the Inland Sea," "Three Naps at Walker Point"

Ploughshares: "August Snow"

Poetry: "A Marriage in Belmont"

Poetry London: "At High Falls," "Liberation in Winter"

The Times Literary Supplement: "Albi"

Tin House: "Parousia"

TriQuarterly: "Autopoiesis," "The Missing"

The Virginia Quarterly Review: "Leaving Hawk Mountain"

Webster Review: "In the Hold"

West Branch: "Exile's Child"

Willow Springs: "The Cave Behind the Torrent"

Yellow Silk: "Late Summer"

Thanks to *The Literary Review* for the Charles Angoff Prize, for work in this book, and to the MacDowell Colony, Yaddo, and the Virginia Center for the Creative Arts.

Thanks to Philip Fried, Hal Sirowitz, Catherine Barnett, Anneliese Wagner, and Richard Hoffman. Special thanks to my editor, Deborah Garrison.

A NOTE ABOUT THE AUTHOR

D. Nurkse is the author of eight previous books of poetry. He has received a Guggenheim Fellowship, the Whiting Writers' Award, two National Endowment for the Arts fellowships, two grants from the New York Foundation for the Arts, a Tanne Foundation award, and two awards from *Poetry* magazine. He has also written widely on human rights. He teaches at Sarah Lawrence College and lives in Brooklyn.

A NOTE ON THE TYPE

THIS BOOK was set in Monotype Dante, a typeface designed by
Giovanni Mardersteig (1892–1977). Conceived as a private type for
the Officina Bodoni in Verona, Italy, Dante was originally cut only
for hand composition by Charles Malin, the famous Parisian punch
cutter, between 1946 and 1952. Its first use was in an edition of
Boccaccio's *Trattatello in laude di Dante* that appeared in 1954. The
Monotype Corporation's version of Dante followed in 1957. Although
modeled on the Aldine type used for Pietro Cardinal Bembo's treatise
De Aetna in 1495, Dante is a thoroughly modern interpretation of the
venerable face.

Composed by Creative Graphics,
Allentown, Pennsylvania
Printed and bound by Thomson-Shore,
Dexter, Michigan
Designed by Virginia Tan